MONUMENTAL MILESTONES
GREAT EVENTS OF MODERN TIMES

The Scopes Monkey Trial

Hundreds of spectators packed the courtroom for the Scopes Monkey Trial.

Mitchell Lane
PUBLISHERS

P.O. Box 196
Hockessin, Delaware 19707

Titles in the Series

MONUMENTAL MILESTONES
GREAT EVENTS OF MODERN TIMES

The Scopes
Monkey Trial

Twenty-four-year old John T. Scopes was the subject of one of America's most bizarre and highly publicized trials.

Jim Whiting

Printing   1   2   3   4   5   6   7   8   9

Library of Congress Cataloging-in-Publication Data
Whiting, Jim, 1943–
    The Scopes monkey trial / by Jim Whiting.
        p. cm. — (Monumental milestones)
    Includes bibliographical references and index.
    ISBN 1-58415-468-3 (library bound)
    1. Scopes, John Thomas—Trials, litigation, etc. 2. Evolution—Study and teaching—Law and legislation—Tennessee—History. I. Title. II. Series.
    KF224.S3W485 2006
    345.73'0288—dc22   2006006100

J 345.73077
S 422

ISBN-10: 1-58415-468-3   ISBN-13: 9781584154686

ABOUT THE AUTHOR: Jim Whiting has been a remarkably versatile and accomplished journalist, writer, editor, and photographer for more than 30 years. He has written and edited about 200 nonfiction children's books. His subjects range from authors to zoologists and include contemporary pop icons and classical musicians, saints and scientists, emperors and explorers. Representative titles include *The Life and Times of Franz Liszt, The Life and Times of Julius Caesar, Charles Schulz, Charles Darwin and the Origin of the Species, Juan Ponce de Leon, What's So Great About Annie Oakley,* and *The Sinking of the* Titanic. He lives in Washington State with his wife and two teenage sons.

PHOTO CREDITS: Cover, p. 6—Getty Images; pp. 1, 3, 10, 21, 24, 25, 33—Library of Congress; pp. 15, 20, 31, 34—Smithsonian Institute Archives; p. 36—*Time.*

PUBLISHER'S NOTE: This story is based on the author's extensive research, which he believes to be accurate. Documentation of such research is contained on page 47.

The internet sites referenced herein were active as of the publication date. Due to the fleeting nature of some web sites, we cannot guarantee they will all be active when you are reading this book.

PLB

Contents

The Scopes Monkey Trial

Jim Whiting

*For Your Information

William Jennings Bryan addresses the jury during the trial.

Bryan was famous as a three-time presidential nominee. He volunteered to help the prosecution in their case against John T. Scopes.

The Trial of the Century

"Civilization is on trial,"[1] said one of the key figures in the courtroom, the most famous criminal defense attorney in the country.

In turn, the chief prosecutor described the defense attorney as "the greatest menace present-day civilization has to deal with."[2]

"It is the first case of its sort since we stopped trying people in America for witchcraft,"[3] retorted the defense attorney.

"The contest . . . is a duel to the death,"[4] responded another prosecutor, a man who nearly became the president of the United States.

With so much at stake, it's no wonder that many people called it the Trial of the Century.

For several weeks in the summer of 1925, the eyes of the nation were directed toward a tiny Tennessee town. Newspapers all across the country reported every development. Many of the country's best reporters provided in-depth analyses. It was the first court case to receive gavel-to-gavel live-broadcast media coverage. Motion picture cameras filmed the highlights to show an anxiously awaiting public.

Unlike modern-day legal spectaculars, the defendant wasn't a prominent politician or a popular media figure. He was a teacher. And he wasn't on trial for murder or another serious charge. In fact, he wouldn't even face jail time if he was convicted. He was charged with a misdemeanor. Misdemeanors are minor offenses such as speeding, public drunkenness, and petty shoplifting. The punishment for most misdemeanors is payment of a fine.

The law this man was accused of breaking was very new. The governor who signed the law doubted that it would ever be enforced. He signed it to gain

support for another law—a new tax on tobacco that would finance far-ranging school reforms.

There wasn't any real doubt about defendant's guilt. In fact, his arrest was almost a lark. He went to court immediately—but it was a tennis court behind the high school where he taught. The city attorneys who began the prosecution were his good friends. Before charging him, they bought him a soft drink.

Some notorious trials are about a conspiracy. That was the case with this one, but the goal wasn't anything sinister. The plotters just wanted to put their small town on the map. Times had been tough, and many people had moved away. The plotters thought that a little publicity might attract out-of-town investors. They hatched their plan in one of the local drugstores.

When word of the upcoming court case began to circulate, newspapers all over the country were incredulous. Virtually no one had ever heard of the town. Editors had to comb through their atlases with magnifying glasses to pinpoint its location.

Although the location was obscure, the subject of the trial attracted some heavy hitters. A three-time presidential candidate volunteered to help the prosecution. The country's most famous criminal attorney led the defense. A fledgling civil liberties organization in New York City saw a perfect opportunity to gain invaluable publicity for itself. Even the presiding judge wanted to spend time in the spotlight.

When it was over, both sides claimed victory. Historians have endlessly debated the outcome, but the consensus is that neither side won. The issue that caused the trial—the teaching of the theory of evolution in public schools—still dominates national headlines.

Officially the trial was known as the *State of Tennessee v. John T. Scopes.* Its unofficial nickname has become far more famous: the Scopes Monkey Trial.

Charles Darwin

Charles Darwin left England on the ship *Beagle* in 1831. He was a somewhat aimless young man who thought he might become a minister. When he returned after nearly five years of sailing around the world, he had found his purpose in life. During the long voyage, he saw a great deal of the natural world. He sent back many specimens from his travels. Along with his notes, these established him as a serious scientist.

He thought a lot about what he had seen and began developing a theory of evolution. He knew it would be controversial. He did a lot of research to support his conclusions.

He finally published a book about evolution in 1859. Entitled *On the Origin of the Species*, it threw the literal interpretation of the Bible into question. According to the Book of Genesis, all forms of life were created within a span of a few days. They were also created in exactly the form in which we see them today.

Darwin disagreed. He theorized that the earth was far older than many people believed. Living things had changed a great deal during that time. They had "evolved" into their present forms.

The cornerstone of the theory was "natural selection." Darwin said small changes called mutations helped some members of a species adapt better to their surroundings, increasing their chances of survival. For example, some giraffes developed longer necks than others, which made it easier for them to get food. They were better suited to their environment. Over the course of many generations, all giraffes would come to have long necks.

While Darwin shied away from the question of human evolution, his enemies did not. They accused him of saying that humans descended from apes. Gradually the opposition decreased. By the time Darwin died in 1882, his theory had become widely accepted. He was buried in Westminster Abbey, one of England's most important churches.

Defense Attorney John R. Neal (left) Scopes.

Neal was a law professor at the University of Tennessee. He volunteered to represent Scopes, but played only a minor role in the actual trial.

CHAPTER 2

The Tennis Court

On the afternoon of May 5, 1925, a Tennessee high school general science teacher and football coach named John Scopes was playing tennis with some of his students. Classes at the school, located in the small town of Dayton, had ended a few days earlier.

It had been the first year of teaching for the twenty-four-year-old Scopes. He was very popular with his students. On numerous occasions, he allowed them to skip mandatory—and boring—school assemblies. They would slip downstairs to his basement classroom, where Scopes would listen to them talk.

As the match progressed, Scopes noticed a boy patiently waiting at the side of the court. During a break, the youngster approached him. Several men wanted to talk to him, the boy said. They were at the drugstore. Still sweating in the spring heat, Scopes followed the boy.

He had just taken the first steps on a path to immortality.

In 1686, English scientist Isaac Newton formulated his Third Law of Motion: For every action there is an equal and opposite reaction.

That was certainly the case following the publication of Charles Darwin's book, *On the Origin of the Species*, in England in 1859. The book introduced the theory of evolution. It suggested that the Bible wasn't literally true.

Many ministers were outraged, as were their congregations. They vehemently criticized Darwin and his supporters. Gradually the furor died down as the theory became more accepted. Two prominent clergymen of the Church of England were pallbearers at Darwin's funeral just over twenty years later.

American high schools began teaching the theory of evolution. There was very little opposition. One reason was that relatively few teenagers even attended high school, let alone graduated. As a result, only a handful learned about evolution.

There was another reason. Nearly all high school students in that era were whites, as was the majority of the nation's population. For whites, textbooks came to a comforting evolutionary conclusion. One of the most commonly used editions claimed, "At the present time there exist upon the earth five races or varieties of man, each very different from the others in instincts, social customs, and, to an extent, in structure. . . . The highest type of all [are] the Caucasians, represented by the civilized white inhabitants of Europe and America."[1]

This attitude changed dramatically after World War I. Many other social changes were also occurring. In the decade that began in 1920, people had lots of money to spend. They used it to have a good time. Women, who had gained the right to vote, began dressing in shockingly short skirts. Both sexes drank openly in public—which was illegal. The country had just adopted the Eighteenth Amendment. Also known as Prohibition, the amendment prohibited the manufacture, sale, and transportation of alcoholic beverages. Illegal drinking establishments called speakeasies sprang up all over the country.

Many Christians, particularly those in the southern states, were horrified by what they considered the excesses of the era. They wanted people to return to the fundamental moral teachings of the Bible. They became known as fundamentalists.

The theory of evolution became a primary target of the fundamentalists. By then, many more youngsters were in high school. Their parents thought that learning about evolution would lead to a decline in morals. They wanted schools to stop teaching the theory.

This movement's leading figure was three-time Democratic Party presidential candidate William Jennings Bryan. He believed in the Bible, and that the appalling slaughter in World War I was at least partially a result of teaching evolution. He also believed that the citizens had a right to determine what their children were taught in school. Inspired by his speeches and books, about a dozen states began considering legislation to outlaw the teaching of evolution.

The first state to act was Tennessee. In 1921, a farmer named John W. Butler was shocked by a sermon in the Baptist church he regularly attended. The minister mentioned a young woman who had just returned from college. Her belief in God had been replaced by belief in evolution.

A father of five, Butler didn't like that his children were learning about evolution in school. He decided to do something about it. He ran for the state legislature the following year. Part of his campaign was based on his opposition to teaching evolution.

Early in 1925, during his second term, he introduced a bill that would make it illegal for any public school teacher "to teach any theory that denies the story of the Divine Creation of man as taught in the Bible, and to teach instead that man had descended from a lower order of animal."[2] Anyone found guilty would be fined between $100 and $500.

Butler and his supporters were sincere. As Darwin's great-great-grandson Matthew Chapman points out, "The fundamentalists who tried to banish the theory of evolution did so because they feared it would destroy faith in God and leave only a vacuum in its place."[3]

Losing faith in God was risky. Butler and other fundamentalists preached that the U.S. government was founded on Christian principles. If these principles were called into question, they warned, the very foundation of the government would be threatened. They wanted public schools to teach Christian principles. Evolution, they believed, undermined them.

The Tennessee House of Representatives passed the Butler bill, 71-5, on January 27, 1925, just six days after it was introduced. There had been very little discussion about it.

Reactions were different when the bill reached the state Senate. The quick House vote had caught evolution supporters off-guard. They launched a counterattack. Letters to the editor and editorials appeared frequently. "The quicker this jackass measure is booted into a waste basket, the better for the cause of enlightenment and progress in Tennessee,"[4] wrote one newspaper.

The Senate appeared to agree. A committee rejected the bill, and its passage seemed doubtful. Then both houses took a monthlong recess, providing plenty of time for the antievolution forces to go on the offensive. The pendulum swung in the opposite direction. On March 13, the Senate passed the bill 24-6.

Now it was up to Governor Austin Peay. He had a reputation as a progressive, a person who believed in modern thinking. He also had an ambitious program for modernizing public education in Tennessee. Much of it would be

funded by a tax on tobacco. He knew that powerful interests would oppose this tax. They would put pressure on legislators to vote it down. To keep the legislature on his side, he signed the bill on March 21. A few days later, the legislature passed the tax. The Tennessee public school system could then afford a major overhaul.

Peay downplayed the potential effects of the Butler Act. It "will not put our teachers in any jeopardy," he told the legislature. "I can find nothing of any consequence in the books now being taught in our schools with which this bill will interfere in the slightest manner."[5] He concluded, "Nobody believes that it is going to be an active statute."[6]

Soon afterward, the New York City–based American Civil Liberties Union (ACLU) learned about the passage of the Butler Act. Its members strongly believed in academic freedom and freedom of speech. They believed that the Butler Act threatened these principles.

Though the ACLU had been founded several years earlier, hardly anyone outside of New York had ever heard of it. Now its founder, Roger Baldwin, saw an opportunity to make a name for his organization.

On May 4, the group bought space in many Tennessee newspapers. The notice read, "We are looking for a Tennessee teacher who is willing to accept our services in testing this law in the courts. Our lawyers think a friendly test can be arranged without costing a teacher his or her job."[7]

One interested reader was George Rappleyea. He lived in Dayton, a town about 30 miles northeast of Chattanooga. A mining engineer, he was one of the town's leading citizens. Like many other people in Dayton, he was concerned that the town was declining. It had lost nearly half its population in less than thirty years. By 1925, fewer than 2,000 people lived there.

Rappleyea hurried to Robinson's Drug Store the following day. Owner Fred Robinson also happened to be the president of the local school board. Both men were opposed to the legislation. Excitedly Rappleyea outlined his plan: Find a Dayton teacher who had taught evolution after the law had gone into effect. Put him on trial. Bring in the ACLU, which would pay all the costs of the trial. The trial would attract media attention, which would bring lots of visitors to Dayton. Perhaps it would even attract financial investment.

Robinson didn't need much convincing. He telephoned some of the town's other prominent citizens, asking them to come to the drugstore. One

It was therefore the natural site for the town's leading citizens to confer as they decided how to proceed. They invited Scopes to join them. Then they outlined their plan to him.

Robinson's Drug Store served as a social gathering place for Dayton's townspeople.

was Walter White, the school superintendent. He apparently supported the legislation. He also supported anything that would give publicity to the town. Two of the others were Herbert and Sue Hicks, brothers who were the city attorneys. They agreed to start the prosecution.

Rappleyea explained the urgency of the situation. The notice had appeared all over Tennessee. Dayton had to be the first community to challenge the law. No one would be interested in the second.

The logical candidate was W. F. Ferguson, the principal at Rhea County High School and the school's regular biology teacher. He declined the group's "offer" to serve as the test case. He said that he had to think about his family. He couldn't afford to be fired or fined.

The men moved on to Scopes. They were fortunate he had even spent the last year in Dayton and that he was still there. Scopes was in town as the result of a fluke.

Just before the start of the school year, the general science teacher and football coach had received a better offer elsewhere. The desperate school had to replace him immediately. Scopes was the first man to apply with the proper credentials. He was hired on the spot.

His original plan had been to go back home to Kentucky and sell cars as soon as school let out. A young woman had thrown a wrench into those plans. Scopes met her just before his scheduled departure. He asked if he could see her again. Certainly, she replied—at a church social that was a few days away. His tennis match was one way of killing time while he waited.

Scopes must have been somewhat bewildered when he went into the drugstore. "Robinson offered me a chair and the boy who worked as a soda jerk brought me a fountain drink," he later wrote. " 'John, we've been arguing,' said Rappleyea, 'and I said that nobody could teach biology without teaching evolution.' 'That's right,' I said, not sure what he was leading up to."[8]

The conspirators showed him a section on evolution in *A Civic Biology*, the textbook used in the school. They asked Scopes if he had used the book when he had filled in for Ferguson in April. Scopes replied that he had.

Robinson told him that he had broken the law. Scopes shook his head. He couldn't remember if he had taught that specific section on evolution.

"This did not seem to bother anyone," Chapman writes. "This would do for the moment."[9] It had to. The group didn't have a fallback plan.

Robinson told Scopes about the ACLU proposal. Then he asked, "John, would you be willing to stand for a test case? Would you be willing to let your name be used?"[10]

Scopes didn't have to agree. As Sue Hicks—a close friend of Scopes—later recalled, "After we had discussed that possibility for a while, Scopes said he would be glad to do it, and I said I wouldn't mind to prosecute him."[11]

One reason he accepted was the influence of his father. Thomas Scopes had been a politically active member of a labor union. He stood up for what he believed in. His son, who believed in evolution, would stand up, too.

The men in the drugstore must have breathed a sigh of relief. Scopes was ideal for their purposes. He was young, polite, clean-cut, and well liked in the community. With his horn-rimmed glasses, he appeared to be reasonably intelligent without threatening anyone with radical ideas. He even attended church, though it was more to make friends than because of religious principles.

As soon as Scopes accepted, Rappleyea sent a telegram to the ACLU, taking them up on their offer. Robinson called newspapers in Nashville and Chattanooga, the largest nearby cities. The story appeared the following day. Dayton and John T. Scopes were on the fast track to becoming household names.

On May 9, a preliminary hearing instructed Scopes to appear when the region's grand jury assembled at its usual time in August. Noted law professor John Randolph Neal volunteered to represent Scopes.

Robinson, Rappleyea, and the others were in a great rush. They wanted the trial to begin as soon as possible. They didn't want another community to have an earlier test trial. They were even more upset by Neal's suggestion that the proceedings be transferred to a larger town such as Knoxville or Chattanooga, which would defeat the entire purpose of the plot.

A grand jury was hastily impaneled on May 25 at the Rhea County Courthouse. It was conveniently located across the street from Robinson's Drug Store. Chattanooga judge John T. Raulston presided. Raulston craved publicity. He also viewed the upcoming trial as a way of advancing his conservative Christian beliefs. To no one's surprise, the grand jury indicted Scopes. Raulston set the trial for July 10.

When Bryan heard about the trial, he offered his services to the prosecution. It didn't matter that he hadn't practiced law for more than three decades. He wanted to promote his cause to the entire nation.

Bryan had three primary objections to teaching the theory of evolution. Most important was his belief that the majority of citizens should determine what students were taught in public schools. In this case, he was convinced that the majority wanted their children to learn biblical principles. His second was that if students lost their faith in God, they would become immoral. Third was that he felt evolution had never been proven scientifically.

In Dayton, the conspirators must have rejoiced. Few names were bigger than that of William Jennings Bryan. So far their plan was working.

The ACLU didn't share that feeling. They wanted a narrow constitutional test of the law. Bryan's involvement would broaden the issue. It would become a case of majority rule versus individual rights.

The ACLU suffered a second shock. A famous defense attorney, Clarence Darrow, learned about Bryan's offer. Years before, he and Bryan had been political allies. They had long since split apart. Darrow was an atheist

who was alarmed about the increasing influence of religion in public life. Nearly two years earlier, the front page of the *Chicago Tribune* carried fifty-five questions from Darrow directed to Bryan. The questions dealt with evolution and the Bible. Bryan ignored them.

For Darrow the trial would give him a chance to publicly grapple with Bryan on these issues. He volunteered his services to the defense.

"My object, and my only object, was to focus the attention of the country on the program of Mr. Bryan and the other fundamentalists in America," he later wrote. "I knew that education was in danger from the source that has always hampered it—religious fanaticism. To me it was perfectly clear that the proceedings bore little semblance to a court case, but I realized that there was no limit to the mischief that might be accomplished unless the country was roused to the evil at hand."[12]

As was the case with Bryan, the ACLU knew that Darrow would take the debate beyond the narrow constitutional issues they wanted to raise. Religion itself would be on trial.

In early June, the ACLU invited Scopes to New York. Several prominent legal figures tried to talk him out of using Darrow, saying that Darrow would try to turn the proceedings into a circus. Scopes stuck with Darrow. As author Edward Larson explains, "Facing a criminal prosecution, Scopes wanted an experienced defense lawyer rather than a dignified constitutional attorney. 'It was going to be a down-in-the-mud fight,' [Scopes] recalled, 'and I felt that situation demanded an Indian fighter rather than someone who graduated from the proper military academy.' "[13]

When the trial began, Darrow made his intentions clear. He wanted to show that Bryan and his supporters were a threat to individual liberty. Bryan argued that Christianity and the moral values it emphasized were more essential to the survival of America than Darrow and his atheism.

Bryan often used clever phrases. "It is better to trust in the Rock of Ages [Jesus] than to know the ages of rock,"[14] he told his audiences. It was an obvious slam against the emerging science of geology, which many supporters of evolution used to support their views.

Darrow interpreted the phrase differently. He claimed it made Bryan "the idol of all Morondom. . . . As to science, his mind was an utter blank. . . .

The solid rocks that were laid down millions of years ago meant not a thing to Mr. Bryan."[15]

With the presence of the two heavyweights, national media picked up on the trial. Rappleyea, Robinson, and the other plotters gleefully predicted that up to 30,000 people would descend on Dayton.

The town began to prepare. Some residents departed and rented their homes to visitors. The ones who stayed—as well as some of the newcomers—helped create a carnival-like atmosphere. Banners were everywhere. So, it seemed, were evangelistic preachers speaking out against evolution.

The town wasn't shy about promoting itself. Robinson made a large banner that stretched across the street next to his drugstore. It read: "Robinson's Drug Store: Where It Started."

In the popular imagination, Darwin's theory has always been associated with monkeys and apes, even though this viewpoint isn't very accurate. Dayton capitalized on the idea by importing some chimpanzees. Robinson's chimp appeared in a number of photos. He was shown dressed in a three-piece suit, riding horseback with Robinson's children, and "playing" a tiny piano.

Other Daytonians also played up the monkey theme. Primate pictures appeared in nearly every store window. A town constable put a sign saying Monkeyville Police on the side of his motorcycle. A delivery van became the Monkeyville Express. Sales in stuffed toy monkeys were very brisk.

It didn't take long for what was officially known as the *State of Tennessee v. John T. Scopes* to acquire its famous nickname: the Scopes Monkey Trial, or even just the Monkey Trial.

The citizens knew that most of the big-city reporters thought they were backwoods hicks. Certainly the most famous of them—H.L. Mencken of the *Baltimore Sun*—arrived with that impression. He was pleasantly surprised.

Mencken, who routinely used words such as *imbecile* and *moron* to describe people with whom he disagreed, noted, "The town, I confess, greatly surprised me. I expected to find a squalid Southern village, with . . . pigs rooting under the houses and the inhabitants full of hookworm and malaria. What I found was a country town of charm and even beauty."[16]

Mencken was an exception. Other reporters simply saw what they wanted to see—or what their editors wanted them to see. With their negative

Several Dayton citizens imported chimpanzees to take advantage of the circus-like atmosphere of the trial.

Fred Robinson, the owner of Robinson's Drug Store, photographed this chimp in a variety of situations. By using chimps, Scopes supporters highlighted people's inaccurate ideas about Darwin's theory.

publicity, the primary purpose of the plot had failed. The newspapers were treating both the trial and the town as "a universal joke," as Mencken wrote.

To get even, resentful townspeople played tricks on the reporters. On one occasion, Rappleyea walked into a barbershop. A number of men were just sitting around, talking with each other. Rappleyea began talking about evolution's good features. A man jumped to his feet and shouted, "You can't call my ancestors monkeys!"[17] He chased Rappleyea out the door. On another occasion, a citizen pulled out a gun and fired into the air for no apparent reason. Reporters wrote colorful accounts of these and similar episodes—which had been carefully planned in advance. The townspeople got a good laugh when the reporters thought these bogus events were real.

To Clarence Darrow and William Jennings Bryan, there was nothing funny about what was at stake. They intended to use the trial as a way of spotlighting issues that they believed lay at the very heart of the country's well-being.

Most modern drugstores carry so much merchandise that they can seem like mini department stores. No one would imagine meeting friends there for a pleasant interlude. However, for the men who hatched the idea of arresting John Scopes and prosecuting him, the drugstore was the most logical place to meet. For a number of decades, drugstores were the social centers of their towns. During Prohibition, when bars and taverns were outlawed, drugstores became even more popular.

A drugstore social

The main attraction at the drugstore was the soda fountain. Skilled employees known as soda jerks provided milk shakes, sodas, phosphates (carbonated water and flavored syrups), and other delights for customers. Hardly anyone bought them to go. Instead, they sat down for leisurely conversations at the tables and chairs that took up much of the store's space.

During the trial, a reporter visited Robinson's Drug Store. "Who in all the countryside does not know Robinson's, the social center of this county seat?" he wrote. "Every afternoon, in normal times, the important men of the town drop in for a Coca-Cola and a cigarette. At the little tables they discuss religion, politics and things of local and national importance. . . . The first place any stranger seeks is Robinson's. There he finds all the town celebrities, besides lawyers, reporters, town belles and everybody else."[18]

Hall's Pharmacy in Everett, Washington, opened about the time the Scopes trial began. The founder's grandson, Richard Hall, recalls the wide range of ice cream sodas: vanilla, chocolate, caramel, marshmallow, strawberry, pineapple, cherry, cola, root beer, orange, maple, wild cherry, ginger, mint, and julep. They sold for fifteen cents each. "Twelve choices of 'refreshers' [beverages] were also offered," Hall continues. "The options included Coca Cola at five cents a glass, root beer also priced at five cents, lemonade at ten cents. . . ."[19] Patrons could also order milk shakes, malted milk, and fifteen different ice cream sundaes.

The Rhea County courtroom was packed for the trial.

It was so intensely hot inside, most of the men took their coats off—which was very unusual for the time. Handheld fans were the only means to generate a breeze.

The Trial Opens

At 9:00 A.M. on Friday, July 10, in the second-floor courtroom of the Rhea County Courthouse, Judge Raulston's gavel fell. The Trial of the Century was under way.

A. Thomas Stewart, the regional district attorney, headed the prosecution. Besides Bryan and the Hicks brothers, Stewart's team also included William Jennings Bryan Jr., Dayton attorneys Wallace Haggard and J. Gordon McKenzie, and McKenzie's genial father Ben, who had once held Stewart's position.

Darrow was the big name on the defense team. Arthur Hays, the representative from the ACLU, was the group's chief strategist. The others were Dudley Field Malone, Darrow's friend and a famous attorney in his own right; Neal; and yet another Dayton attorney, Frank McElwee.

The first of an estimated one thousand spectators had begun arriving at least two hours earlier. The lucky ones found seats. The rest had to stand. More than one hundred were reporters. Using four microphones placed around the courtroom, Chicago-based radio station WGN would broadcast the trial to the country. Movie cameras and their operators also competed for space.

The trial coincided with a heat wave. The temperature inside the building may have topped 100 degrees. Opening the windows didn't help very much. Raulston allowed the lawyers to take off their heavy suit coats.

Jury selection went quickly. When the twelve men had been selected, Raulston adjourned the trial for the weekend.

On Monday, before the jury had even been sworn in, Darrow began with a motion to dismiss the charges. Raulston ordered the jurors to leave the room while the legal issues were debated.

A. Thomas Stewart led the prosecution team.

Stewart was probably the most respected figure connected with the trial. The regional district attorney was well-organized and to the point. He later served for ten years in the U.S. Senate.

Arguments back and forth took up the rest of the day. Tuesday began with another defense objection: this time to the traditional Tennessee practice of opening each day in court with a prayer. Raulston overruled the objection.

On Wednesday morning, Raulston took several hours reading his response to the defense motion for dismissal. He refused to grant it.

The "real" trial finally got started that afternoon. Many spectators remembered it as the hottest day of all. With the legal questions finally decided, the jury was allowed to return. Scopes pleaded not guilty to the charge. Chief prosecutor Stewart was a well-organized man. His opening statement consisted of just two sentences. It took less than a minute. In essence, Stewart said that there was a law. John Scopes violated it. In his opinion, it was a very simple case. He called just four witnesses: Superintendent White, Robinson, and two students: fourteen-year-old Howard Morgan and seventeen-year-old Harry Shelton.

Malone's specialty was actually divorce law. He delivered one of the most memorable speeches at the trial. In later life, his law business declined. He became an actor.

Dudley Field Malone was a close friend and associate of Clarence Darrow.

White and Robinson confirmed that Scopes knew that using *A Civic Biology* was a violation of the Butler Act. The two students were there to provide first-hand evidence of Scopes's "crime": that he had actually used the textbook in class.

The lawyers had carefully coached the two boys. For example, Morgan said, "[Scopes] said that the earth was once a hot molten mass too hot for plant or animal life to exist upon it; in the sea the earth cooled off; there was a little germ of one cell organism formed, and this organism kept evolving until it got to be a pretty good-sized animal, and then came on to be a land animal and it kept on evolving, and from this was man."[1] The precise phrasing made it obvious that Morgan had memorized what he had been instructed to say.

When Darrow cross-examined Shelton, he asked the youngster if he left church when Scopes told him that every life-form began with a single cell. Shelton replied that he hadn't.

Outside the courtroom, the mothers of both boys were interviewed. Shelton's mother said, "As far as I'm concerned, they can teach my boy evolution every day of the year. . . . He had forgotten most of his lessons and had to get the book out and study it up."[2]

Morgan's mother expressed similar feelings.

When the two boys left the witness stand, Scopes was finally able to relax. A few days later, he made an astonishing confession to reporter William K. Hutchinson: "I didn't violate the law. . . . I never taught that evolution lesson. I skipped it. I was doing something else the day I should have taught it"—according to some sources, he was diagramming plays for the football team—"and I missed the whole lesson about Darwin and never did teach it. Those kids they put on the stand couldn't remember what I taught them three months ago. They were coached by the lawyers. Honest, I've been scared all through the trial that the kids might remember I missed the lesson. I was afraid they'd get on the stand and say I hadn't taught it and then the whole trial would go blooey. If that happened they would run me out of town on a rail."

When Hutchinson replied that would make a great story, Scopes said: "My god no! Not a word of it until the Supreme Court passes my appeal. My lawyers would kill me."[3]

William Jennings Bryan was born in Salem, Illinois, in 1860. By a bizarre coincidence, Scopes moved to Salem when he was a boy and graduated from the same high school as Bryan. Even more coincidentally, the two men met when Bryan delivered the address to Scopes's graduating class.

After moving to Nebraska and serving as a lawyer for several years, Bryan was elected to Congress in 1890. Establishing a reputation as someone who cared for ordinary people, he acquired the nickname the Great Commoner. He supported progressive ideas such as a graduated income tax and women's right to vote.

He believed firmly in religious values. His most famous speech, given at the 1896 Democratic Party presidential convention, was pep-

William Jennings Bryan

pered with religious imagery: "You shall not press down upon the brow of labor this crown of thorns; you shall not crucify mankind upon a cross of gold."[4] At that time, the U.S. dollar was supported only by gold. Bryan wanted to add silver, a much more common metal, to the treasury. Adding silver would have extended wealth to many more people.

The speech catapulted him from obscurity to the nomination. His proposal threatened people with established wealth. In what was the country's first "big-money election," these people donated huge amounts of cash to his Republican opponent, William McKinley. McKinley won. Bryan's defeat also dragged down a Democratic congressional candidate, Clarence Darrow.

Bryan ran again in 1900 and 1908. He lost both times. He became secretary of state when Woodrow Wilson won the presidency in 1912. It was his highest public office.

His opposition to the theory of evolution was consistent with his political philosophy. At the time of the trial, many people believed in a form of evolution known as Social Darwinism, or "survival of the fittest." People in power used it to justify their position. They said they were the strongest and didn't owe anything to anyone else. Bryan thought if he could establish traditional Christian values of caring for one another, the misery of common folk might be reduced or even ended.

Clarence Darrow (left) and William Je share a moment during the trial.

Though they appear cordial, the two men were actually bitter enemies. At one point they had been good friends, but political and religious differences drove them apart.

The Defense Strikes Back

The defense had assembled a stable of high-powered scientific talent. It wasn't difficult. Some of the country's best-known scientists wanted to come to Dayton. They shared Darrow's concern that science itself was on trial. Maynard Metcalf, a professor of zoology at Johns Hopkins University in Baltimore, was the first one to take the stand.

Stewart objected. The issue was not the theory of evolution, but whether Scopes had broken the law. Darrow replied that the law only forbade instruction that specifically denied the Biblical account of creation. Metcalf and the others would testify that Christianity was compatible with the theory of evolution.

Raulston hesitated. Again he excused the jury. Metcalf was allowed to continue, though no one was sure why. The reporters and the spectators were the only people who were listening to Metcalf's testimony. They weren't the ones who would determine Scopes's guilt or innocence.

On Thursday, Stewart objected to using any more of the expert witnesses. Bryan rose in support. To this point, he had remained largely silent. Now he delivered a long, somewhat rambling speech. The courtroom was packed. Thousands more were outside, listening through loudspeakers. As author Paul Conkin notes, "He ended with paeans of praise for the Bible and with the simple question at stake in the trial: Did Scopes violate an act that may have displeased the so-called experts but clearly reflected the wishes of the vast majority of Tennesseans?"[1] The applause was thunderous.

Malone responded. Many on both sides—including Bryan himself, who called Malone's the best speech he had ever heard—thought it was the high point of the trial. He raised the crucial point that in order for Scopes to be found guilty, the prosecution had to prove that Scopes had taught that man

descended from lower animals and that the theory of evolution was contradictory to the Bible. He conceded that they had proven the former. They hadn't done so with the latter. "If what Scopes taught was, according to the understanding of the ablest minds in the country, consistent with a proper use and understanding of the Bible, then Scopes was not guilty."[2]

Stewart may have been impressed with the speech, but he remained adamant: no expert witnesses. The arguments continued for the rest of the day.

Friday's court session lasted just over an hour—enough time for Raulston to explain that he would not admit the testimony of any expert witnesses. If he had granted the defense motion, the prosecution was prepared to import its own set of expert witnesses. Once that happened, the trial could go on for weeks. He did make one concession: the defense witnesses could provide brief summaries in the official record of what their arguments would have been.

After Raulston's ruling, many reporters concluded that the trial was over. It appeared that Scopes would be found guilty. They headed home. So did some of the key figures, such as William Jennings Bryan, Jr. He and the rest of the prosecution team believed they had won.

They missed out on one of the most famous scenes in American trial history. It came on Monday when the trial moved outside. An inspection of the first-floor ceiling in the courthouse during the weekend revealed several cracks from the weight of all the bodies and equipment that had been crammed into it. They couldn't use the rooom.

First, Darrow won a rare victory from the judge. He objected to a large sign posted nearby that said, "Read Your Bible." Darrow wanted equal time. He proposed putting up a sign saying, "Read Your Evolution." Raulston ordered the Bible sign taken down.

Then Darrow resorted to a very unusual strategy. He called Bryan to the stand as an "expert witness" on the Bible. Stewart objected. Bryan shrugged Stewart off. He felt equal to anything that his opponent could ask. It was what both of them wanted: a chance to finally go one-on-one, with much of the nation as witnesses. Besides, he was under the impression that he would get equal time to publicly question Darrow and other defense lawyers.

Rappleyea had conceived the idea of putting a Dayton teacher on trial for violating the Butler Act. He had recently moved to Dayton from New York. Like Scopes, he didn't stay in Dayton long when the trial ended.

Scopes (left), attorney John Neal (center), and George Rappleyea ignore a Read Your Bible sign.

For nearly two hours, Darrow hammered Bryan with relentless questions about the Bible. Most of the reporters thought Darrow was the clear winner, while many Christian groups gave the nod to Bryan. For example, one group claimed that Bryan won 70 percent of the exchanges, Darrow won 20 percent, and the remaining 10 percent were a draw.[3]

No one doubts the dislike that each man felt for the other.

Darrow said, "You insult every man of science and learning in the world because he does believe in your fool religion. . . . I am examining you on your fool ideas that no intelligent Christian on earth believes."[4]

Bryan fought back. "The only purpose Mr. Darrow has is to slur at the Bible," he said. "The only reason [Darrow] asked any question is . . . to give this agnostic an opportunity to criticize a believer in the word of God; and I answered the question in order to shut his mouth so that he cannot go out and tell his atheistic friends that I would not answer his questions."[5]

Under the constant barrage of questions, Bryan sometimes admitted that he didn't accept parts of the Bible as literal. Those responses dismayed many fundamentalists. Sometimes he even appeared to trip over his own words, as in the following exchange from the trial transcript:

Q (Darrow)—"What do you think?"
A (Bryan)—"I do not think about things I don't think about."
Q—"Do you think about things you do think about?
A—"Well, sometimes."
(Laughter in the courtyard.)
Policeman—"Let us have order."[6]

The humorous jabs weren't one-sided. At one point, Darrow asked Bryan, "Where have you lived all your life?"
Bryan responded, "Not near you."[7]
It was great theater, but it had little bearing on the actual case. The following morning, Judge Raulston threw out the entire exchange. Darrow asked the judge to bring in the jury and instruct them to deliver a "guilty" verdict. Legally, it wasn't an admission of guilt. It would, however, provide the basis for the appeal that the defense had wanted all along.
It also accomplished two other things. Bryan wouldn't get to put Darrow on the stand and question him. Nor would he get to deliver the lengthy closing argument he had written.
It took the twelve men just nine minutes to return a guilty verdict. Raulston told the jury that they could assess the fine or they could leave it to him. They let him do it. Judge Raulston fined Scopes $100. It was the lowest possible amount he could have assessed. Almost as an afterthought, the judge asked Scopes if he had anything he wanted to say.
It was an unusual invitation. With so many high-powered agendas in operation, Scopes had long since become an odd man out. He never took the stand on his own behalf. One day during the noon recess, he went swimming in with William Jennings Bryan Jr. and returned a few minutes late. Hardly anyone noticed his absence. He even filled in for a reporter who had become ill, in effect writing about his own trial.

Darrow's intentions extended far beyond the twelve men in the jury box. He wanted them to find Scopes guilty. Then he could appeal the verdict. He hoped that he could carry his appeal all the way to the U.S. Supreme Court.

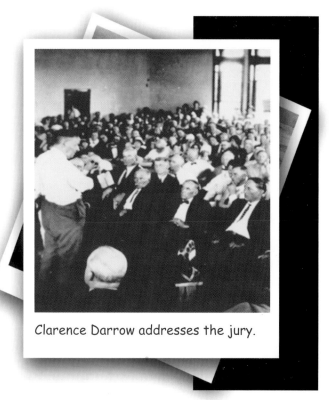

Clarence Darrow addresses the jury.

A few days after the trial ended, he found out just how anonymous he had been. He had briefly left Dayton and was returning. He and a reporter shared a taxi. The driver had no idea who they were. At one point, the taxi waited to cross the Tennessee River on a ferry. As they prepared to board, they saw the people coming from the Dayton side getting off the boat. The driver recognized one and pointed him out to Scopes and the reporter.

As Scopes recalled, "The driver said, 'You know who that was? That was Judge Raulston who was the Judge in that 'Monkey Trial.' I wish I was in his place; I would have seen that Scopes, Darrow and all of the rest of those damn atheists got tarred and feathered and railed out of the State.' He talked the rest of the way to Dayton. I found out, in no uncertain words, what some people thought of my colleagues and me."

As he got out of the vehicle at the end of the ride, Scopes introduced himself. The driver was shocked to learn who his passenger had been. "If I had

After the trial moved outdoors, Darrow (right) questioned Bryan (seated facing him at the left).

The interchange between the two lawyers was one of the most famous parts of the trial, but it had no effect on the outcome. The judge struck it from the official record.

not moved quickly, I might have been killed, he made his getaway so fast,"[8] Scopes said.

With the eyes of the court finally on him, Scopes responded. "Your Honor," he said, "I feel that I have been convicted of violating an unjust statute. I will continue in the future, as I have in the past, to oppose this law in any way I can. Any other action would be in violation of my ideal of academic freedom—that is, to teach the truth as guaranteed in our Constitution of personal and religious freedom. I think the fine is unjust."[9]

Most of the remaining lawyers made brief statements. Judge Raulston expressed his appreciation of the way that the trial had gone. A local clergyman delivered a brief benediction. Everyone began streaming out of the courtroom. It was time for lunch.

The Scopes Monkey Trial was over. The issues it raised would not be so quickly resolved.

Clarence Darrow

Clarence Darrow was born in 1857 in Ohio. His father was an atheist, which was unusual for that era. The family took the same nonreligious position. Darrow worked as a small-town lawyer, then moved to Chicago in 1890 to assume a high-paying position with a railroad. That job came to an abrupt end during a railroad strike. Darrow was horrified to learn that the company had simultaneously lowered wages and increased the rent in company-owned housing. Darrow resigned. He sided with the strikers and defended some of them in court.

That led to a number of other high-profile cases. In 1911, he defended two men who were accused to dynamiting the offices of the *Los Angeles Times* newspaper. He was accused of trying to bribe jurors. The accusations weren't proved.

By then he had developed his public image. He tried to come across as a "just folks" kind of man, one who didn't care about wearing good clothes. Beneath the

Richard Loeb and Nathan Leopold

shabby exterior lay a sharp legal mind with exceptional speaking skills. He needed both in 1924 when he defended Richard Loeb and Nathan Leopold, two brilliant young men from wealthy families. Wanting to commit a perfect crime, they kidnapped a boy and murdered him. There was no doubt about their guilt. Darrow saved them from the death penalty, to which he was adamantly opposed.

Soon after the Scopes Trial, Darrow became involved in the Dr. Ossian Sweet case. Sweet was an African American who moved into a white area in Detroit. His neighbors demanded that he move out. A mob attacked his home. Sweet and his friends shot at the attackers. One of the attackers was killed. A trial ended in a hung jury. A second trial focused on Dr. Sweet's brother Henry. Darrow successfully defended him—a remarkable achievement at a time when African Americans were still being lynched in relatively large numbers.

Shortly afterward, Darrow retired. He died in 1938.

An August 2005 Time magazine cover reveals that the issues raised by the Scopes Trial are still very much alive. Americans remain divided about whether or not evolution should be taught in schools. The debate seems likely to continue for a long time.

Scopes II, III, and So On

After the trial, both sides claimed victory. Many people have seen either the film or stage version of *Inherit the Wind*, which is based on the Scopes Trial. Some teachers suggest that students watch the film to learn the basic facts. However, *Inherit the Wind* takes many liberties with the actual events. One is the premise that the defense won.

In reality, there was no consensus which side was the actual "winner" at the time. In 1999, one reporter concluded, "The passage of time has obscured one important result from the infamous Scopes 'Monkey Trial': No one is sure who won."[1]

"Not a single [newspaper] editorial at the time determined it was a decisive event either killing the anti-evolution crusade or a tremendous victory propelling it,"[2] adds Edward Larson.

For the ACLU, the trial achieved the group's objective: publicity. Even though many people disagree with its methods and the cases in which it chooses to become involved, the ACLU remains an important voice in American public life.

The trial also affected the teaching of evolution. In its immediate aftermath, many science teachers simply avoided the subject. This trend has continued into the 21st century.

"In districts around the country, even when evolution is in the curriculum it may not be in the classroom, according to researchers who follow the issue," noted *New York Times* reporter Cornelia Dean in 2005. "Teaching guides and textbooks may meet the approval of biologists, but superintendents or principals discourage teachers from discussing it. Or teachers themselves avoid the topic, fearing protests from fundamentalists in their communities."[3]

Darrow did get his way—sort of. According to plan, the verdict was appealed to the Tennessee Supreme Court. Arguments began in May 1926. The following January, the court made its ruling. The law was constitutional. However, it threw out Scopes's conviction on a technicality: The jury, rather than the judge, should have set the amount of the fine. Then the court dismissed the case, commenting, "Nothing is to be gained by prolonging the life of this bizarre case."[4]

Darrow was outraged. He wanted the case to go all the way to the U.S. Supreme Court, where the arguments about evolution and religion would be conducted on a national stage. He couldn't appeal a case that had been dismissed. The Butler Act remained in force until 1967, when the Tennessee legislature repealed it. No one besides John Scopes was ever prosecuted under its terms.

By then, nearly all the major figures had died. Five days after the trial, Bryan died in Dayton of a heart attack. He assumed almost saintlike status among his followers. Many believed that he had given his life in defending the Christian religion. A few years later, a Bible-oriented school now named Bryan College opened in Dayton to honor his memory and maintain his principles.

Governor Peay died two years after the trial. He too was honored with an institution of higher learning. What is now Austin Peay State University was established in 1927 in Clarksville.

While Peay's political career came to a premature end, Tom Stewart's was just beginning. He later became a U.S. Senator from Tennessee.

Judge Raulston didn't fare as well at the ballot box. He was defeated for reelection in 1926.

One minor legacy of the affair arose from attorney Sue Hicks. He became the inspiration for the 1969 Johnny Cash song "A Boy Named Sue."

Darrow was involved in a few more important cases after the Scopes Trial. When he retired, he was invited to return to Dayton to receive an award. He noticed a new church near the hotel where he was staying. "Well, I didn't do much good here after all,"[5] he joked.

The new church was a fitting symbol for Dayton. The town has remained true to its fundamentalist roots. It has experienced modest growth—its population is about 6,000 people. The descendants of several trial figures

still live there. In many respects, it seems little changed by its brief encounter with fame.

Yet it can never escape that encounter. The town hosts a three-day festival in July that includes daily staged highlights from the trial. The Scopes Museum is located in the Rhea County Courthouse. Robinson's Drug Store is long gone, but a plaque showing its location remains.

John Scopes became an instant celebrity. Many people in his position would have cashed in on their fame. Scopes didn't. "Many times I have been asked why I have had no further role to play relative to the issues—even why I did not at least capitalize on my publicity and reap the monetary harvest that was close at hand. Perhaps my best answer is to paraphrase Calvin Coolidge's 'I do not choose to run,' for me it would be, 'I did not choose to do so.' "[6]

Scopes would never teach public school again. Though the Dayton school board offered him his job back—as long as he agreed not to teach evolution—he declined. Prominent scientists around the nation passed the hat on his behalf. They contributed enough money for him to attend graduate school at the University of Chicago. He earned a degree in geology and became a petroleum engineer.

John wasn't the only Scopes to leave the teaching profession in 1925. His sister Lela was fired from her job teaching mathematics in the family's hometown of Paducah, Kentucky. Part of the reason was her brother's notoriety. Part was her refusal to deny the theory of evolution.

Rappleyea, whose sharp eyes and civic booster spirit had begun the entire affair, didn't stay long in Dayton either. He invested in business ventures in Cuba, Canada, and other parts of the United States. He died in 1967.

Scopes never had hard feelings toward Dayton. He had planned on frequently visiting the many friends he had made during his year of teaching there. His career intervened. Much of it was centered in Venezuela, where no one had heard of him. He finally returned in 1960 to promote the film version of *Inherit the Wind*. The town's leaders declared the occasion as Scopes Trial Day and presented him with a key to the city.

In 1967, he published his autobiography, *Center of the Storm*. He was characteristically modest. "I furnished the body that was needed to sit in the defendant's chair," he noted. "A man's fate is often stranger than anything the imagination may produce."[7]

The following year, the U.S. Supreme Court finally ruled on the issues that Darrow had hoped to raise in 1925. In *Epperson v. Arkansas*, the Court ruled against the Arkansas statute forbidding the teaching of evolution in public schools, finding it went against the First Amendment. It was also deemed to be in violation of the Fourteenth Amendment.[8] Darrow would have been delighted.

About that decision and others similar to it, Scopes noted, "I feel that restrictive legislation on academic freedom is forever a thing of the past, that religion and science may now address one another in an atmosphere of mutual respect and of a common quest for truth. I like to think that the Dayton trial had some part in bringing to birth this new era."[9]

Scopes proved to be an inaccurate prophet. "Restrictive legislation" has not gone away—at least not in the United States. If anything, the controversy about teaching evolution became even more heated at the close of the twentieth century and the start of the twenty-first. Numerous public statements and court cases have only served to widen the divide between the two sides.

Because of the Epperson decision, public schools can't teach the biblical version of creation. The next theory proposed to counter Darwin was that of Intelligent Design (ID). ID maintains that there are serious flaws in Darwin's theory. It also maintains that the universe is too complicated to have evolved by mere chance. It must have been created by a higher power. Its advocates stop short of saying that this higher power is God.

Intelligent Design became the focal point of a celebrated court case in 2005. The previous year, the Dover County (Pennsylvania) school board adopted a requirement that science teachers must state that Darwin's theory of evolution is not an established fact and explain that Intelligent Design is one alternative. It was probably the first such requirement in the country. Backed by the ACLU, a group of parents protested. They maintained that Intelligent Design is religiously based and therefore violated the constitutional separation of church and state. The combination of religion and evolution and some close parallels with the 1925 trial led some observers to nickname it Scopes II.

As the *New York Times* pointed out, "For years, a lawyer for the Thomas More Law Center in Michigan visited school boards around the country searching for one willing to challenge evolution by teaching intelli-

gent design, and to face a risky, high-profile trial."[10] That action was similar to what the ACLU had done in 1925.

Another parallel is that the case went beyond what the instigators had anticipated. "The school district never consulted us and did the exact opposite of what we suggested," said John G. West, a senior fellow at the Discovery Institute, an organization in the forefront of the Intelligent Design movement. "Frankly I don't even know if school board members know what intelligent design is."[11]

A few days before the end of 2005, U.S. District Judge John E. Jones III handed down his decision. The judge agreed with the parents who opposed the requirement. "Our conclusion today is that it is unconstitutional to teach ID as an alternative to evolution in a public school science classroom,"[12] he wrote in his 139-page opinion.

The decision was something of an anticlimax. More than a month earlier, Dover County citizens had voted all eight members of the school board out of office. Their replacements abolished the requirement early in 2006.

The Dover election was part of a flurry of evolution-related news that occurred at about the same time. On November 8, 2005, the Kansas state board of education adopted new standards that question the scientific validity of evolution. The decision was consistent with published reports that the majority of Kansas citizens want other theories besides evolution to be taught, and that at least a third feel the Biblical story of creation offers the best explanation for the way in which life began.

The day before the Kansas decision, one of the most important officials in the Catholic Church issued his own opinion. "Cardinal Paul Poupard, head of the Pontifical Council for Culture, said the Genesis description of how God created the universe and Darwin's theory of evolution were 'perfectly compatible' if the Bible were read correctly," noted journalist Martin Penner. "His statement was a clear attack on creationist campaigners in the U.S., who see evolution and the Genesis account as mutually exclusive."[13]

The Scopes Monkey Trial is therefore the first—and the most famous—salvo in a battle that continues to dominate news headlines. Scopes III, IV, V and perhaps even more seem inevitable in the years to come.

In the early 1950s, Jerome Lawrence and Robert E. Lee wrote a dramatized version of the Scopes Trial called *Inherit the Wind*. In 1960, Hollywood got into the act. Many people believe that *Inherit the Wind* is an accurate depiction of the trial. It isn't.

At the beginning, Scopes is arrested in his classroom and thrown in jail. In reality, Scopes never spent a moment behind bars. The film takes further liberties with the facts, such as changing the names of major characters and introducing several fictional ones. The Darrow character is more heroic in the film than he was in real life. The Bryan character becomes a fanatical buffoon, and he dies of a heart attack during the trial. Very little dialogue actually comes from the trial transcript.

Lawrence and Lee weren't trying to deceive people. As they explained, *"Inherit the Wind* is not history. . . . Some of the characters of the play are related to the colorful figures in that battle of giants; but they have life and language of their own—and, therefore, names of their own."[14]

The authors aren't entirely correct. Their play *is* about history—just not the history of the Scopes Trial.

In the early 1950s, the nation's intellectual freedom came under attack. In a series of televised hearings, U.S. Senator Joseph McCarthy warned that many Americans, including some in the U.S. government, were communists. The threat was greatly exaggerated, but McCarthy became such a powerful figure that few had the courage to stand up to him. The careers of many innocent people were ruined.

"Lawrence and Lee used the Scopes Trial, then safely a generation in the past, as a vehicle for exploring a climate of anxiety and anti-intellectualism that existed in 1950,"[15] says the University of Missouri Scopes Trial website.

Actor Tony Randall, who starred in the original Broadway play, agrees. *"Inherit the Wind* was a response to and a product of McCarthyism . . . the authors looked to American history for a model."[16]

Chronology

1923	Clarence Darrow poses 55 questions about the Bible and evolution to William Jennings Bryan in the *Chicago Tribune*; Bryan refuses to respond.
1925	
January 21	John Washington Butler introduces legislation into the Tennessee Legislature that would prohibit teaching that humans evolved from lower animals.
January 27	Tennessee House of Representatives passes the Butler Act.
March 13	Tennessee State Senate passes the Butler Act.
March 21	Tennessee Governor Austin Peay signs the Butler Act into law.
April	John Scopes allegedly violates the Butler Act.
May 4	American Civil Liberties Union (ACLU) runs newspaper advertisements offering free legal support for anyone teaching evolution in Tennessee.
May 5	Dayton civic leaders meet in Robinson's Drug Store; John Scopes agrees to serve as defendant in a test case of the Butler Act.
May 25	A local grand jury indicts Scopes.
July 10	*State of Tennessee v. John T. Scopes* trial begins; jury is selected.
July 15	Prosecution rests after an hour of testimony; defense opens with introduction of expert witness Maynard Metcalf.
July 16	Bryan and defense attorney Dudley Field Malone deliver speeches to great applause.
July 17	Judge John Raulston rules that defense cannot use testimony of expert witnesses.
July 20	Darrow puts Bryan on the witness stand.
July 21	Scopes is found guilty and is fined $100.
July 26	Bryan dies in Dayton.
1926	Scopes guilty verdict is appealed to the Tennessee Supreme Court.
1927	The Tennessee Supreme Court rules that the Butler Act is constitutional but overturns Scopes's conviction on a technicality, which ends further court challenges to the verdict.
1967	Tennessee repeals the Butler Act.

Timeline in History

1831   Charles Darwin leaves England on round-the-world voyage on the *Beagle*.

1857   Clarence Darrow is born in Kinsman, Ohio.

1859   Darwin publishes *On the Origin of the Species*.

1860   William Jennings Bryan is born in Salem, Illinois.

1882   Darwin dies.

1896   Bryan runs for U.S. President; he also runs in 1900 and 1908 but loses all three times.

1900   John T. Scopes is born in Paducah, Kentucky.

1914   World War I begins; George William Hunter publishes *A Civic Biology*.

1918   World War I ends.

1919   The 18th Amendment to the U.S. Constitution is ratified; it forbids the manufacturing and transportation of liquor and begins the era of Prohibition.

1920   Women in the United States gain the right to vote with the passage of the 19th Amendment.

1921   William Jennings Bryan becomes a leader in the antievolution movement, delivering speeches such as "The Menace of Darwinism" across the country.

1926   Mississippi becomes the second state to ban the teaching of evolution.

1927   Hunter publishes *A New Civic Biology*, which deals with the concept of evolution cautiously and avoids using the word *evolution*.

1929   The stock market crashes, plunging the United States into the Great Depression.

1930   William Jennings Bryan University (now Bryan College) opens in the Rhea County High School in Dayton.

1933   Franklin D. Roosevelt is elected U.S. President as he promises a "New Deal" for Americans; 21st Amendment repeals the 18th and ends the era of Prohibition.

1938   Clarence Darrow dies.

1970   John Scopes dies.

1972   Rhea County Courthouse (The Scopes Museum) is designated a National Historic Landmark.

2004   School board in Dover County, Pennsylvania, orders high school biology teachers to provide warnings about the theory of evolution and mention Intelligent Design as an alternative; some parents object and go to court in what some media call Scopes II.

2005   Dover County voters unseat entire Dover school board; a federal judge overturns warning requirement; Kansas State Board of Education mandates standards that compel science teachers to include criticisms of biological evolution along with evidence for it.

2006   Several candidates run for election to Kansas State Board of Education with the intention of changing the standards passed the previous year in favor of evolution.

Chapter Notes

Chapter 1   The Trial of the Century

1. "State v. John Scopes ('The Monkey Trial')." http://www.law.umkc.edu/faculty/projects/ftrials/scopes/evolut.htm
2. "A. Thomas Stewart." http://www.law.umkc.edu/faculty/projects/ftrials/scopes/stewarts.htm
3. Edward J. Larson, *Summer of the Gods* (New York: Basic Books, 1997), p. 193.
4. Ibid., p. 143.

Chapter 2   The Tennis Court

1. Andrew Bradbury, "The Scopes Monkey Trial," http://www.bradburyac.mistral.co.uk/tenness7.html
2. Edward J. Larson, *Summer of the Gods* (New York: Basic Books, 1997), p. 50.
3. Matthew Chapman, *Trials of the Monkey: An Accidental Memoir* (New York: Picador USA, 2000), p. x.
4. Larson, p. 52.
5. Ibid., p. 58.
6. Ibid., p. 59.
7. Chapman, p. 30.
8. Larson, p. 89.
9. Chapman, p. 30.
10. Larson, p. 90.
11. Larson, p. 91.
12. Clarence Darrow, *The Story of My Life* (New York: Da Capo Press, 1996), p. 249.
13. Larson, p. 102.
14. Doug Linder, "Famous Trials in American History: Tennessee vs. John Scopes— The 'Monkey Trial,' 1925," copyright 2002, http://www.law.umkc.edu/faculty/projects/ftrials/scopes/scopes.htm
15. Darrow, pp. 249–250.
16. H.L. Mencken, "The Monkey Trial—A Reporter's Account," http://www.law.umkc.edu/faculty/projects/ftrials/scopes/menk.htm
17. Steve Kemper, "Evolution on Trial," *Smithsonian*, April 2005, p. 57.
18. American Experience—Monkey Trial, "People and Events: The American Drugstore," http://www.pbs.org/wgbh/amex/monkeytrial/peopleevents/e_drugstore.html
19. Richard Hall, "Stanton Hall and Hall's Pharmacy of Everett," March 23, 2004, http://www.historylink.org/essays/output.cfm?file_id=5656

Chapter 3   The Trial Opens

1. "Scopes Trial, Day 4," http://www.law.umkc.edu/faculty/projects/ftrials/scopes/day4.htm
2. Doug Linder, "John Scopes," http://www.law.umkc.edu/faculty/projects/ftrials/scopes/SCO_SCO.HTM
3. David N. Menton, Ph.D., "Inherently Wind: A Hollywood History of the 1925 Scopes 'Monkey' Trial," http://www.gennet.org/facts/scopes.html
4. Doug Linder, "William Jennings Bryan," http://www.law.umkc.edu/faculty/projects/ftrials/scopes/bryanw.htm

Chapter 4   The Defense Strikes Back

1. Paul Conkin, *When All the Gods Trembled* (Lanham, MD: Rowman and Littlefield Publishers, 1998), pp. 90–91.
2. Ibid., p. 91.
3. Richard M. Cornelius, "World's Most Famous Court Trial," http://www.bryan.edu/802.html
4. "Scopes Trial, Day 7" http://www.law.umkc.edu/faculty/projects/ftrials/scopes/day7.htm
5. Ibid.
6. Ibid.
7. Edward Caudill and Edward Larson and Jesse Fox Mayshark, *The Scopes Trial: A Photographic History* (Knoxville: The University of Tennessee Press, 2000), p. 17.
8. John Thomas Scopes, "Reflections on the Scopes Trial," http://www.law.umkc.edu/faculty/projects/ftrials/scopes/scopesreflections.html
9. "Scopes Trial, Day 8" http://www.law.umkc.edu/faculty/projects/ftrials/scopes/day8.htm

Chapter 5   Scopes II, III, and So On

1. ABCNews.com, "Rethinking the Scopes Trial," September 19, 1999, http://abcnews.go.com/sections/science/DailyNews/scopestrial990919.html
2. Andrew Bradbury, "The Scopes Monkey Trial," http://www.bradburyac.mistral.co.uk/tennesse.html
3. Cornelia Dean, "Evolution Takes a Back Seat in U.S. Classes," *The New York Times*, February 1, 2005, http://aolsvc.news.aol.com/news/article.adp?id=20050201100909990010&_ccc=3&cid=842

4. "Decision on Scopes' Appeal to the Supreme Court of Tennessee." http://www.law.umkc.edu/faculty/projects/ftrials/scopes/statcase.htm

5. Steve Kemper, "Evolution on Trial," *Smithsonian*, April 2005, p. 58.

6. John Thomas Scopes, "Reflections on the Scopes Trial," http://www.law.umkc.edu/faculty/projects/ftrials/scopes/scopesreflections.html

7. Doug Linder, "John Scopes," http://www.law.umkc.edu/faculty/projects/ftrials/scopes/SCO_SCO.HTM

8. Susan EPPERSON et al., Appellants, v. ARKANSAS. No. 7. Supreme Court of the United States; Argued October 16, 1968; Decided November 12, 1968, http://www.law.umkc.edu/faculty/projects/ftrials/conlaw/Epperso.htm

9. Scopes, "Reflections."

10. Laurie Goodstein, "In Intelligent Design Case, a Cause in Search of a Lawsuit," *The New York Times*, November 4, 2005, http://www.nytimes.com/2005/11/04/science/sciencespecial2/04design.html?ex=1131771600&en=022c31a8fa8af523&ei=5059&partner=AOL

11. Ibid.

12. *Associated Press*. "Court Rejects 'Intelligent Design' in Science Class." December 20, 2005, http://nullbull.gnn.tv/headlines/6711/Court_rejects_intelligent_design_in_science_class

13. Martin Penner, "Evolution in the Bible, Says Vatican," *The Australian*, November 7, 2005, http://www.news.com.au/story/0,10117,17162341-13762,00.html

14. Andrew Bradbury,"Inherit the Wind—It Wasn't," http://www.bradburyac.mistral.co.uk/tenness2.html

15. "Notes on Inherit the Wind." http://www.law.umkc.edu/faculty/projects/ftrials/scopes/SCO_INHE.HTM

16. Edward J. Larson, *Summer of the Gods* (New York: Basic Books, 1997), p. 240.

Glossary

agnostic (ag-NOS-tik)
A person who doubts the existence of a god or gods.

atheist (AY-thee-ist)
A person who is convinced that god or gods do not exist.

belles (bells)
Pretty girls.

benediction (BEN-eh-dik-shun)
A prayer asking for God's blessing.

evangelistic (ee-van-juh-LIS-tik)
Trying to obtain commitments to Jesus as Christ.

indicted (in-DY-tid)
Formally charged with committing a crime.

paeans (PEE-uns)
Joyous songs, honors.

pallbearers (PAWL-bayr-urs)
People who carry the coffin at a funeral.

squalid (SKWAH-lid)
Especially dirty or filthy.

Further Reading

For Young Adults

Hanson, Freya Ottem. *The Scopes Monkey Trial*. Berkeley Heights, NJ: Enslow Publishers, 2000.

Kidd, Ronald. *Monkey Town: The Summer of the Scopes Trial*. New York: Simon and Schuster Children's Publishing, 2006.

Kraft, Betsy Harvey. *Sensational Trials of the Twentieth Century*. New York: Scholastic Press, 1998.

Nardo, Don. *The Scopes Trial*. San Diego: Greenhaven Press, 1997.

Olson, Steven P. *The Trial of John T. Scopes*. New York: Rosen Publishing Group, 2004.

Whiting, Jim. *Charles Darwin and the Origin of the Species*. Hockessin, DE: Mitchell Lane Publishers, 2005.

Works Consulted

Caudill, Edward, and Edward Larson and Jesse Fox Mayshark. *The Scopes Trial: A Photographic History*. Knoxville: The University of Tennessee Press, 2000.

Chapman, Matthew. *Trials of the Monkey: An Accidental Memoir*. New York: Picador USA, 2000.

Conkin, Paul K. *When All the Gods Trembled*. Lanham, MD: Rowman and Littlefield Publishers, 1998.

Darrow, Clarence. *The Story of My Life*. New York: Da Capo Press, 1996.

Kemper, Steve. "Evolution on Trial." *Smithsonian*, April 2005, pp. 52–61.

Larson, Edward J. *Summer of the Gods*. New York: Basic Books, 1997.

On the Internet

Adams, Noah. "Timeline—Remembering the Scopes Monkey Trial," NPR, July 5, 2005, http://www.npr.org/templates/story/story.php?storyId=4723956

American Experience—Monkey Trial http://www.pbs.org/wgbh/amex/monkeytrial/

Associated Press. "Court Rejects 'Intelligent Design' in Science Class." December 20, 2005, http://nullbull.gnn.tv/headlines/6711/Court_rejects_intelligent_design_in_science_class

Associated Press. "Robertson: God May Smite Down Town That Voted Out Anti-Evolution School Board." November 11, 2005. http://www.foxnews.com/story/0,2933,175247,00.html

Bradbury, Andrew. The Scopes Monkey Trial. http://www3.mistral.co.uk/bradburyac/tennesse.html

Cornelius, Richard M. "World's Most Famous Court Trial." http://www.bryan.edu/802.html

David N. Menton, Ph.D. "Inherently Wind: A Hollywood History of the 1925 Scopes 'Monkey' Trial." http://www.gennet.org/facts/scopes.html

Dean, Cornelia. "Evolution Takes a Back Seat in U.S. Classes." *The New York Times*, February 1, 2005. http://aolsvc.news.aol.com/news/article.adp?id=20050201100909990010&_ccc=3&cid=842

Gibson, L. James. Inherit the Wind—Revisited http://www.grisda.org/origins/51046.htm

Goodstein, Laurie. "In Intelligent Design Case, a Cause in Search of a Lawsuit." *The New York Times*, November 4, 2005. http://www.nytimes.com/2005/11/04/science/sciencespecial2/04design.html?ex=1131771600&en=022c31a8fa8af523&ei=5059&partner=AOL

Hall, Richard. "Stanton Hall and Hall's Pharmacy of Everett." http://www.historylink.org/essays/output.cfm?file_id=5656

Linder, Doug. "Famous Trials in American History: Tennessee vs. John Scopes—The 'Monkey Trial,' 1925." http://www.law.umkc.edu/faculty/projects/ftrials/scopes/scopes.htm

Penner, Martin. "Evolution in the Bible, Says Vatican." *The Australian*, November 7, 2005. http://www.news.com.au/story/0,10117,17162341-13762,00.html

Reflections on the Scopes Trial by John T. Scopes http://www.law.umkc.edu/faculty/projects/ftrials/scopes/scopesreflections.html

Index